DIGGING DEEPER INTO THE PAST
THE ROMANS

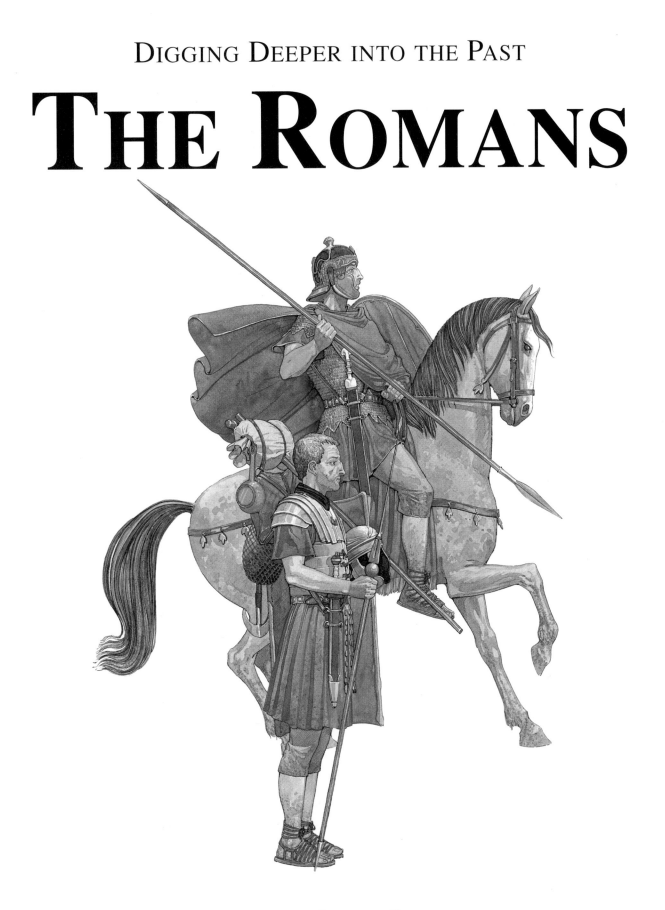

JOHN AND LOUISE JAMES

Heinemann

ACKNOWLEDGEMENTS

The publishers would like to thank John Orna-Ornstein for his advice and assistance in
the preparation of this book, and the organizations that have given their permission to
reproduce the following pictures:

AKG Photo, London: 8 (fresco).
Ancient Art & Architecture Collection: 10 (dogs), 24 (lamp), 25 (mosaic), 26 (boots).
Bath Archaeological Trust: 14 (mask).
Bayerisches Landesamt Für Denkmalpflege/K. Leidorf: 6 (fort).
Courtesy of the Trustees of the British Museum: 6 (diploma), 8 (figurine), 11 (slave tag),
12 (gaming pieces), 13 (strigils), 14 (bronze boar), 16 (ploughman), 18 (mould), 19 (pendant), 23 (wheel), 25 (figure), 28 (medallion).
Colchester Museums: 10 (figures).
C.M.Dixon: 21 (relief).
Deutsches Bergbau-Museum, Bochum/Astrid Opel: 22 (miners).
English Heritage, Chesters Museum: 16 (measure).
Gloucester City Museum: 26 (gravestone).
Robert Harding Picture Library: 28-29 (Trajan's column).
Michael Holford: 9 (inkpot).
Landesmuseum, Trier: 16-17 (relief).
Musée de Bourges: 19 (gravestone).
Musée Fenaille-Rodez, collection Société des Lettres, Sciences et Arts de l'Aveyron) © Gilles Torjeman: 19 (tally).
Museum of London: 13 (strigils and jars), 20 (coin), 20 (vase).
Rheinisches Landesmuseum, Mainz: 26 (dagger in scabbard).
Scala Fotografico: 8 (bracelet), 8 (glassware), 9 (doll), 15 (altar), 24-25 (relief), 26 (sword), 29 (standard).
Service Photographique de la Reunion des Musées Nationaux: 14-15 (relief).
St Albans Museum: 15 (figurine).
Yale University Art Gallery/courtesy Oxford University Press: 6 (letter).

Written by: Louise James
Illustrated by: John James
Editor: Andrew Farrow
Design: John James and Alec Slatter
Art Director: Cathy Tincknell
Production Controller: Lorraine Stebbing
Consultant: John Orna-Ornstein

First published in Great Britain in 1997
by Heinemann Children's Reference,
an imprint of Heinemann Educational Publishers,
Halley Court, Jordan Hill, Oxford, OX2 8EJ,
a division of Reed Educational & Professional Publishing Ltd.

MADRID ATHENS PARIS
FLORENCE PORTSMOUTH NH CHICAGO
SAO PAULO SINGAPORE TOKYO
MELBOURNE AUCKLAND IBADAN
GABORONE JOHANNESBURG KAMPALA NAIROBI

ISBN 0431 05322 7

A CIP catalogue record for this book is available at the British Library.

Printed and bound in Italy

CONTENTS

This scene of a busy market shows Romans and Celts going about their daily business. How typical is it of Roman life?

SETTING THE SCENE

FRANCE AD 150

According to legend, the city of Rome was founded in 753 BC. Through the efforts of its people and the conquests of its army, it became a great empire that lasted for hundreds of years. The empire was vast, with frontiers as far north as Britain, west into Portugal, south into Africa and east to parts of Asia. There the Romans took their way of life, language and their culture. They also adapted and adopted the cultures and religions of the peoples they now ruled, and even made some of them Roman citizens.

Hadrian's Wall

MARE GERMANICUM (GERMAN SEA)

BRITANNIA

Londinium (London)

GERMANIA

Aquae Sulis (Bath)

OCEANUS ATLANTICUS (ATLANTIC OCEAN)

Lutetia (Paris)

GALLIA (GAUL)

Lugdunum (Lyon)

Arretium (Arezzo)

Narbo (Narbonne)

Massilia (Marseilles)

Roma (Ron

HISPANIA

(Rio Tinto)

(Valverde)

Gades (Cadiz)

Key to map: Olive oil · Wine · Pottery · Wheat
Gold · Glass · Ivory · Wool

ABOUT 850 BC GREECE EMERGES FROM DARK AGES   ABOUT 753 BC FOUNDATION OF ROME   332 BC EGYPT FALLS TO ALEXANDER THE GREAT   140 BC GREECE FALLS TO ROMAN ARMIES

EGYPT

GREECE

ROMANS

1000 BC   500 BC   0

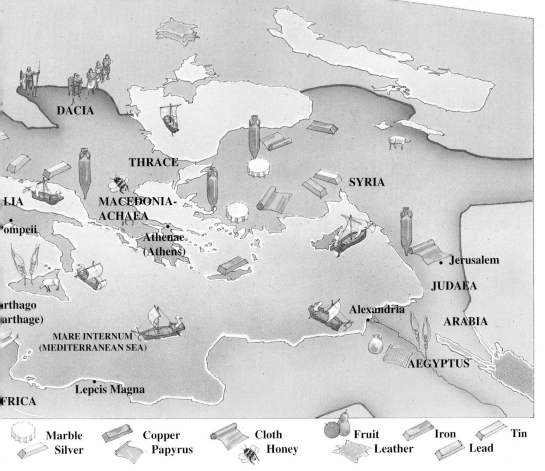

DACIA

THRACE

SYRIA

MACEDONIA-
ACHAEA

...LIA

...ompeii

Athenae
(Athens)

Jerusalem

JUDAEA

Alexandria

ARABIA

...arthago
...arthage)

MARE INTERNUM
(MEDITERRANEAN SEA)

AEGYPTUS

Lepcis Magna

...FRICA

Marble   Copper   Cloth   Fruit   Iron   Tin
Silver   Papyrus   Honey   Leather   Lead

For many people Roman rule was harsh and cruel, for others it was a time of wealth and achievement. Architects and engineers built monuments, roads and temples. Statesmen ruled huge provinces, and improvements were made in farming and industry, such as setting up some of the first factories.

This book looks at a selection of the evidence for the Roman way of life, including written accounts, pottery, wall paintings and monuments. Some are being discovered even as you are reading. Using the exciting things that have been found, we can unravel the mystery of our past, to reveal much about the Roman way of life.

The map shows the Roman Empire in about AD 100. It also shows some of the main goods traded by the Romans.

The timeline below shows when the Romans lived in comparison to some other important civilizations.

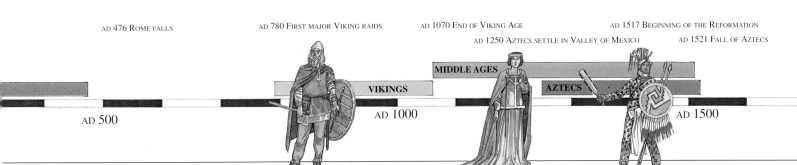

AD 476 ROME FALLS

AD 780 FIRST MAJOR VIKING RAIDS

AD 1070 END OF VIKING AGE

AD 1517 BEGINNING OF THE REFORMATION

AD 1250 AZTECS SETTLE IN VALLEY OF MEXICO

AD 1521 FALL OF AZTECS

MIDDLE AGES

VIKINGS

AZTECS

AD 500

AD 1000

AD 1500

HISTORY IN EVIDENCE

How do we know about the Romans? We have learned much about their way of life because archaeologists and historians study the things that have survived from past times. They are very much like detectives, looking for evidence and working out how and why things happened.

Some information comes from books written by Roman citizens. The politician and warlord Julius Caesar wrote about the wars he had fought in. Others described the common events of daily life. For example, the writer Juvenal described a street in the city of Rome in the second century AD:

'However fast we hurry there's a huge crowd ahead and a mob behind pushing and shoving... You get dug in the ribs by someone's elbow... The streets are filthy – our legs are plastered with mud, someone tramples your feet, or a soldier's hob-nailed boot lands right on your toe.'

This photograph shows the remains of a Roman fort. Archaeologists use aerial photographs of the area they will be working on. From the air it is often possible to see the outlines of buildings demolished long ago.

Written evidence such as diaries and military records help us to understand the lives of the Romans. Above is part of a letter found in North Africa, telling of a reception for an important visitor. Left is a bronze diploma giving a soldier an honourable discharge from the Roman army.

Archaeologists use a variety of tools in their work, from digging tools and trowels, like those shown on the left, to pencils, paper and lap-top computers for recording finds. There are hundreds of Roman sites that have not yet been studied.

Sometimes an object, like this pottery jar called an amphora, is found intact. More often it has broken into many pieces. Occasionally these pieces can be put back together to show the shape of the original object.

Archaeologists usually study the places where people lived and worked. Before 'digging' begins, accurate details of a site are taken, including photographs at ground level and from the air. Sometimes, special electronic surveys are also carried out, as they can detect things hidden underground, such as a ditch or stone wall. As the site is 'dug', everything that is found is recorded and labelled. Each item can give clues to the uses of rooms and buildings, and about who lived there.

The soil taken from an excavation is checked in case any small items have been missed. Microscopic examination of the soil can also show what type of plants grew in it, what animals there were and even the food that people ate.

The style of buildings has changed as new civilizations have built on top of earlier sites, especially towns and cities. Here we can see a range of buildings from an ancient Bronze Age hut to a modern block of offices.

Type I, until AD 90

Type II, AD 40-100

Type III, AD 70-200

Type IV, AD 150-400

Typology is the study of how the design of an object changes over time. This builds up a sequence that can be used to date other artefacts. Above is a sequence of oil lamps and their main periods of use.

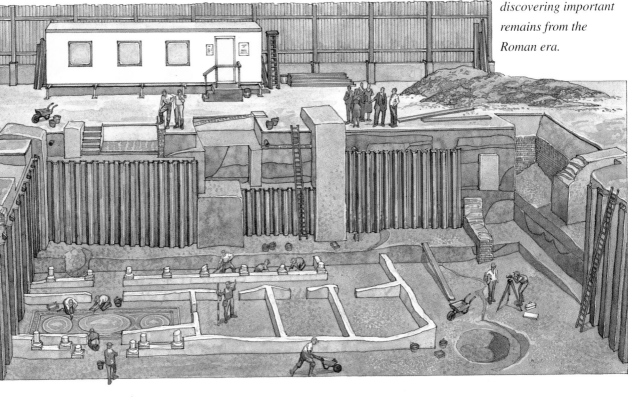

Below we can see an archaeological dig in progress. The dig is discovering important remains from the Roman era.

ROMANS AT HOME

FRANCE AD 180

In the Roman Empire, the sort of home people lived in depended on whether they were rich or poor. In a Roman city or town, poorer people lived in blocks of flats called *insulae* (islands), which were three or four storeys high. The flats were always crowded and often dirty. Two whole families, maybe more, might be squashed in a single room.

Rich people and the patricians, the Roman nobles, had magnificent homes. They had their own bathrooms, piped water and many luxuries. Some people lived in town houses. Others, who lived out in the country, had villas, like the one shown on the right. The main entrance led into a reception room called an *atrium*. The *atrium* often had beautifully carved columns and a pool called an *impluvium* in the middle.

Family life centred around the *atrium*. Doors off it might lead into a dining room, the kitchen, bedrooms and maybe a library. Families kept a small shrine with a statuette of their *lar familiaris*, their guardian spirit (below right). Every day, the family said prayers at the shrine.

The writer Juvenal said that the ideal Roman mother (shown in this fresco from Pompeii) had to be hardworking, loyal to her husband and family, and make sure the home was a comfortable and happy place to be.

The houses of wealthy Romans were full of treasures such as the lustrous glassware (right), brightly-coloured pottery, or jewellery made from gold or silver, like the serpent bracelet on the left. Jewellery was often decorated with portraits of people. Ordinary people, the plebeians, could not afford things like these.

The marble floors of villas were covered in beautiful mosaics (above) made from tessarae, *tiny pieces of stone or coloured glass (see page 21).*

The scene on the left shows some of the people in a wealthy family. The father, seated, was the *paterfamilias*, Latin for 'father of the family'. Children had to obey their father without question. The mother was also important: she was in charge of the smooth running of the household. Just as the father trained the boys, the mother trained the girls. Each delegated, or gave, work to servants.

Some of the people working in Roman families did not want to be there. These were the men, women and children who had been sold as slaves. In the middle of the first century AD, there were millions of slaves in Italy. Slaves did all kinds of work – as servants in private homes, labourers on farms, or oarsmen in Roman ships.

In colder areas, the walls of some villas were made hollow so that heat from the hypocaust (below), the heating system beneath the house, could warm the rooms. A fire was lit in the basement, and the heat travelled up through the walls.

Children played with toys that are still popular hundreds of years later. This wooden doll had movable arms and legs, with metal pins to attach them to the body. Female dolls had their own sets of clothes.

The Romans did not use much furniture, but it was often decorated, perhaps with carved legs (above and right). Couches were covered with padded cushions to make reclining comfortable.

One of the family's most trusted servants kept the household records, using an inkpot and pen like these.

IN THE GARDEN

Near the centre of each villa was a garden. The garden was an important place where the family could relax. Sometimes it was also used as a summer dining room. In the picture on the right we can see an informal meal being enjoyed by the family and their guests. This is probably the main meal of the day, which might start in the afternoon and last late into the evening.

Roman diners did not sit on chairs, but reclined on couches. We also know, from written sources and archaeological evidence, what types of food and drink were popular. The empire was vast, so there was a wide choice of food and fine wines for the few who could afford them. However, most people ate simple dishes with strong tasting sauces like *garum*, a fish sauce. A Roman meal was not hurried, as people took time to enjoy the many courses. Meal time was meant to be a social event, and politics, business and art were often discussed.

Below is a large bronze jug. The base of the handle is in the shape of a man's head, with flowing hair and long beard.

These amusing terracotta (clay) people were found in a child's grave. One of them is telling a story to the other diners.

Wealthy diners used things made by the finest craftsmen, like the terracotta dish and plate (top), the bronze spoon (above) and the silver dish and plate (left).

The Romans kept dogs as pets and as guard dogs. This marble statue (above) comes from Italy.

Below is a slave tag, which was lost until discovered by archaeologists. It reads 'Hold me lest I flee, and return me to my master Viventius on the estate of Callistus'.

These keys, found in a Roman garden, were for locking away the family's valuables.

The dig (left) shows the discovery of an outdoor dining area in France. Only in warm climates did people dine outside.

Diners ate and drank while laying on couches arranged around three sides of a table. A good host might entertain his guests with dancing and music played on instruments like these bronze cymbals, flute and bell (left).

The garden was a beautiful place, with flowers, trees, a fountain and ornate walkways. Sometimes walls were decorated with paintings called frescos, which were painted directly on to the plaster. Many show scenes of the gods or animals, or beautiful patterns. The Romans also painted their statues, although the paint has now worn away.

The children of the household are not present at the meal. Perhaps they are at a small private school or are being taught at home, by a slave who had been well educated himself. Not all children had the chance to be educated. Many children who were poor, or even slaves, had to work long hours.

AT THE BATHS

The Romans were a very clean people. Many of them bathed daily at the public baths, the *thermae*, which were not very expensive to use. But the baths were not just for getting clean, they were like a club where people could get together to relax and enjoy themselves. They swapped news and jokes, discussed business matters, placed bets on wrestling matches or chariot races, played games, or exercised hard in a gymnasium. The writer Lucius Seneca described some of the people at one bath-house:

'First there are the "strongmen" doing their exercises... with grunts and groans. Next there are lazy ones having a massage... And what about the ones who leap into the pool making a huge splash as they hit the water!'

The baths were a place for socialising. People met there to relax, talk and enjoy themselves. These counters, knuckle bones and dice would have been used in a variety of games. Gambling and betting, although not officially legal, were common.

Busy towns had two or three public baths, some small, some large. Most baths had a hypocaust system to heat the water, floors and air. Hot air from a furnace was channelled under the floor and up through spaces in the walls.

Men and boys usually bathed at different times to women and girls. As foaming soap had not been invented, people cleaned their bodies by pouring perfumed oil or a soap made from tallow (animal fats) onto their skin. They would perhaps exercise then relax in a warm pool called a *tepidarium*. Later they would move to the hot and steamy *caldarium*, where the heat opened the pores of the skin, and then scrape off the oil and dirt using a curved tool called a *strigil*. After a swim in a hot pool, the bather would plunge in a cold pool (the *frigidarium)* to close the skin's pores.

Left, this green glass flask probably held a perfumed oil which was rubbed into the body after bathing. Below is a bronze toilet set, with a nail cleaner and tweezers. Most bathers had their own set.

Below are an ear scoop, tweezers and a nail cleaner. In the scene a bather is using a scoop to clean out his ear.

Below right are an oil flask and strigiles. *Baths had many slaves to scrape the customers clean and serve food and drink.*

The remains of Roman baths can be found in places like Bath in southern England. Bath was known as Aquae Sulis in Roman times. The ruined baths were discovered and restored in the 19th century (left).

The bronze dish (left) was used for pouring water over a bather. Sometimes the floor beneath bathers' feet was so hot they had to wear wooden clogs, called pattens (above).

Sacrifice at the Temple

North Africa AD 125

The Romans worshipped many gods. They thought that each god influenced certain aspects of the world, and each would help them in specific areas of their lives. For example, people who were ill or infirm prayed to Asclepios, the god of healing.

Everyone had to worship the official Roman gods. Most official gods were the same as Greek gods, but known by different names. The Greek god of war, Ares, was known as Mars, Aphrodite became Venus, and the father of the gods, Zeus, became Jupiter. However, as their empire expanded, the Romans happily adopted the beliefs and honoured the gods of the people they conquered, such as the Egyptian god Isis and the Persian god Mithras.

The Romans built magnificent temples for their gods. Many were dedicated to just one god, though some large temples such as the Pantheon in Rome were for several. Sometimes a special day was dedicated to a god. This day was treated as a holiday and there would be a festival.

The larger-than-life tin mask below was found in a spring. It was probably used in a sacrificial ritual.

At a sacrifice, large animals were killed with an axe. A knife (above) was used to slit open the animal's stomach, then its entrails would be put in the bowl. The jug would have held wine as an offering to a god.

This bronze model shows a man leading a boar to be sacrificed. The animal will be cut open so its entrails can be burned and examined for omens.

The Persian god Mithras (top) became popular among slaves and soldiers. Priests of Mithras sacrificed bulls in secret ceremonies. The goddess Venus, above, was associated with gardens, beauty, love and fertility.

On the left is part of a marble relief from Rome showing a sacrifice to the god Mars. Altars were often decorated, such as the one in Rome's main forum, above.

In the scene above, priests are sacrificing live animals on an altar outside a temple. People believed that sacrificing animals pleased the gods.

In the first century AD, Christianity became popular. Christians worship only one god and follow the teachings of Jesus Christ. This brought them into conflict with the emperors, who thought this would anger Rome's official gods and bring ill-fortune to the empire. The Christians were forced to worship in secret and many were persecuted. For example, the emperor Nero outlawed them and treated them as criminals. Some were paraded in the amphitheatre and forced to battle with wild animals.

FIRE AT THE BAKERY

One of the most important foods was bread. Freshly baked bread was part of most Romans' daily diet, so in every town there was at least one bakery. There wheat was ground by huge stones called querns. Then the bread was made and baked in ovens, before being sold at the shop counter.

Wheat for bread making was grown in many parts of the empire. Every year, the emperor had to import shiploads of wheat from Egypt to feed the poorer people of Rome. If the grain ships did not arrive in time, the people might riot. The army, too, needed wheat, to feed its soldiers, and so it controlled many farms. Other large farms were owned by wealthy nobles who had hundreds of slaves to prepare the soil, plant seeds and harvest the crops.

A shortage of water could be a big problem for farmers. Therefore the Roman army built waterways, called aqueducts, to take water to the places it was needed, and the farmers were able to irrigate (water) the land.

As the bronze model shows, the design of ploughs used by the Romans remained virtually unchanged until replaced by modern machinery. The sickle shown on the right would have been used to cut down the fully grown wheat.

On the right is the top part of a quern, which was used to grind wheat into flour. Every farm and estate would have had one.

Above, this bronze model shows oxen pulling a plough. The farm worker, who is wearing a hooded cloak, is guiding the cattle and plough.

Sometimes farmers had to give part of their harvest to the army, especially when the legions were fighting a long campaign. On the left is a first century bronze corn measure used to collect this corn levy (tax), called the annona.

The German relief above shows bakers preparing and mixing their ingredients and baking bread. Most bakeries had a mill room. The grain was poured into the top of the quern, then the upper stone was turned to grind the grain into flour.

The scene above shows a bakery that has caught fire. A fire in a large timber-framed building could spread quickly and burn down the whole town. Here the townsmen are filling their buckets from a water trough. Fires were such a problem in Rome that in AD 6 the emperor Augustus created a group of fire-fighters called the *vigiles*. The *vigiles* were freed slaves who won the right to citizenship after six years' service.

This loaf of bread was found at Pompeii in Italy, buried by ash when the volcano Vesuvius erupted.

Tradesmen used a tool called a steelyard (above) to weigh corn and wheat. The item was hung on one of the hooks, and the weight on the left was moved along the bar until it balanced the load. The tray on the left was used for baking small buns.

Romans paid for goods with coins. Each had the head of the emperor on one side. It could take many years for new coins to circulate to the distant provinces.

THE POTTER'S WORKSHOP

FRANCE AD 175

Many things that we use today are made from glass, metal or plastic. In Roman times they were made from pottery. For storing food, large jars with narrow necks kept food or liquid cool and fresh. People ate from pottery plates, and lit their homes using oil lamps made from clay.

A master potter could produce a range of items, from luxury goods to everyday cooking and drinking vessels. He would have learned about potting by serving an apprenticeship with an experienced craftsman.

Sometimes a pottery was a small family business. Other potteries were large workshops that could produce thousands of items in a week. In a large workshop, the master potter's assistants were slaves who worked hard, in dirty conditions and for long hours.

The mould above was used for making terracotta statuettes of a female figure. It is about 30cm high.

Right is a model of a mime artist holding a bag of money. Actors are usually shown wearing masks.

For about 2,000 years this flask in the shape of a rabbit has survived unbroken. It once contained soothing ointment.

The excavation above shows the remains of a kiln found at Narbonne in southern France. Roman potteries were some of the world's first factories.

This terracotta ink pot (above left) has three small holes in the top, so it can be hung up. Below it are some marbles for children to play with.

This small pendant, made from a black stone called jet, shows two cupids making a pot.

Above is a gravestone from France. The hanging pots show that the man was either a potter in his shop or a merchant selling pottery on a market stall.

There were many forms of pottery in the Empire. Here are a third century Casterware beaker (left) and a Samian bowl and jug (below).

SEXTIMA

OGISK

Each potter put their trademark on their work (above left). Most marks were made by pressing a carved wooden block into the wet clay.

The clay used for potting varied from region to region, and this meant that many types of pottery, or ware, were produced. At Arretium (Arezzo) in Italy and Lugdunum (Lyon) in France, a shiny red pottery commonly known as Samian ware was made. The pots, which often had raised patterns on them, were usually formed in a mould. The mould was stamped with designs carved from wooden blocks. Samian ware was very popular and was exported throughout the empire.

The pots were fired (heated) in an oven called a kiln. Most pots were not decorated, but some were covered with coloured glazes made with powdered glass and fired again.

Left is a potter's tally (list) from France. The plate lists the names of potters, type of pottery and number of items that were fired – an incredible 27,945!

THE SINKING SHIP

BRITAIN AD 210

In AD **43 the Romans invaded England. Soon the town of Londinium (London) became an important and busy port, visited by ships and merchants from many parts of the empire.**

The town's river banks were lined with quays and small warehouses for storing goods. Ships took the goods around the coast to other ports, and also from country to country. Their cargoes included building materials, tin, wheat, pottery, wine and olive oil. One quay-side site was used for bottling fish, perhaps for making the popular fish sauce called *garum* (see page 10).

In the River Thames at London, the wreck of the Roman trading vessel shown in the scene has been found by archaeologists (above). The timbers had been burrowed into by shipworm, so we know that the boat often sailed at sea.

Above, this coin was found in the socket of the ship's mast. It features the goddess Fortuna, and would have been put there as a good luck token.

The remains of several ships and their cargo have been found in the River Thames, including this Samian vase.

These iron nails were bent to hold the ship's overlapping planks together. The cone heads were hollow, which is very unusual.

As trade increased, the River Thames became crowded with vessels, all trying to get into the safe channels. But sailing was never easy, even in the calm conditions of the river. In the scene on the left we can see how, in a mist, a trading ship has been rammed by another boat. The ship is loaded with a heavy cargo of building stone, which has moved in the collision, and it is capsizing and sinking rapidly. The sailors, some of whom are slaves, are desperately trying to swim away before they are sucked under.

Archaeologists have found the remains of this ship in waterlogged silt, which preserved the wood, European oak, from rotting. The cargo included an unfinished millstone from Yorkshire, over 300 kilometres to the north.

Using a method of studying wood called dendrochronology, the ship has been dated to AD 140. Microscopic study shows that a variety of both fresh and sea water bacteria had lived in the timbers, so we know that the ship travelled widely, perhaps as far as the Mediterranean Sea.

Italy, 1st century

Above are small pieces of coloured stone called tessarae, *used for making mosaics. These pieces were found inside an amphora in a ship wrecked in the Mediterranean Sea.*

Sailors used iron boat-hooks like the one above to pull boats to the quays alongside the river.

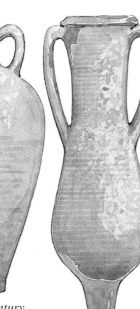

Southern Spain, 1st-3rd century

Gaul, 1st-2nd century

Spain, 1st century

Above are four types of amphorae. They are of a similar style, but with variations in size and type of handle. The jars were used to store or carry goods such as wine or olive oil.

Sometimes amphorae are found with traces of their original contents. Scientists can work out where the goods came from and therefore how widespread and common a trade was.

This third century relief (right) shows clerks recording the number of amphorae being unloaded from a ship in the Italian port of Ostia.

DOWN THE MINE

SPAIN AD 250

The emperors paid for the Roman army, which conquered new lands and defended the frontiers. They ordered lavish games to keep the people entertained. The government built thousands of magnificent buildings, temples and baths. So where did they find the money to do all of this?

Some money came from conquest and taxes. The rest came from businesses owned by the government, such as the trade in grain and metals. Mining was important throughout the empire. In Greece, lead and silver were often found in the same mines – the lead was used for making water pipes, the silver for coins and jewellery. Other important metals and minerals were iron, copper, tin, gold and marble.

Below we can see archaeologists discovering the remains of a wooden waterwheel in a Spanish copper mine. Some waterwheels were made like model kits, ready to be assembled at the mines. In Spain, the skeletons of 18 miners killed and buried by a rock fall have also been found.

This stone carving shows Spanish miners going to work. They are wearing leather aprons and carrying hammers, picks and oil lamps.

22

Iron ankle restraints were used to stop slaves escaping. This one (right) still holds the remains of a slave's foot!

Slaves had to power wooden waterwheels like this one found in a copper mine at Rio Tinto in Spain. The wheels scooped up water and lifted it out of the galleries.

Above are an iron hammer and pick, and two buckets, one made from wood and woven grass, the other from bronze.

This force pump was found in a mine at Valverde in Spain. Like all machinery in the mines, it was powered by slaves. It was probably used to pump fresh water to the workers.

This small bronze figurine of a young slave was found in England. She has been tied by a rope at the neck, wrists and ankles, making it impossible for her to escape.

The mines were planned carefully by engineers who surveyed the landscape and designed ways of getting the valuable materials out of the ground. They also used complex machinery to remove water, to prevent flooding. In the scene on the left an engineer is surveying a new tunnel using an instrument called a *groma*. Below him, slaves are driving waterwheels. The wheels are lifting water into troughs and up to the surface, so the mine doesn't flood.

Most of the hard work was done by slaves, who had to toil in cold, dirty and dangerous conditions. In the 1st century BC, the historian Diodorus Siculus described slaves in a mine:

'... as a result of their underground excavations day and night they become physical wrecks, and because of their extremely bad conditions the mortality [death] rate is high.... Some...prefer dying to surviving.'

AT THE RACES

LIBYA AD 118

All Romans enjoyed their public holidays. They flocked to the theatre to cheer or jeer at the latest comedy. At the huge amphitheatres they watched bloodthirsty gladiators fighting each other to the death. But perhaps the most popular entertainment was chariot racing at the circus. Spectators betted on the outcome and shouted wildly as their favourite team careered round the course.

The huge racing track was long and narrow. Along its centre, the *spina*, or spine, were statues of gods, seating for the marshals or judges, and the lap counters. At the ends were huge columns which marked the turning point. Remains of the circus at Lepcis Magna in Libya show that three cones nearly 5 metres tall (far right) stood at each end of the *spina*.

This Roman lamp, made in Italy about AD 30-70, shows a victorious charioteer holding a palm leaf.

Our evidence of chariots includes this chariot pole end (far right) and a bronze model of a two-horse chariot (above).

The relief above shows chariots racing at the Circus Maximus in Rome. Nothing survives of the Circus Maximus, but there are many remains at Lepcis Magna in Libya. The scene at the top of the page shows the starting gates at Lepcis Magna, which were about 3m wide. There is some evidence that the gates could be opened simultaneously by pulling a lever.

Chariots burst from the starting gates at Lepcis Magna. One team has broken through the wooden gates and is sweeping its rider out of control. The teams had to race round seven laps of the circus (below), about 7km, before finishing in the straight.

The statesman and writer Cassiodorus told how 'the gates are suddenly opened all at the same time' with a loud snap that could be heard by all the spectators.

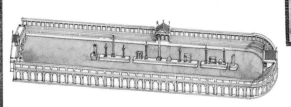

The chariots had two wheels and were very light. They were usually pulled by four horses, but sometimes by just two. Like many modern sports teams, some chariot-racing teams had their own 'supporters' clubs' and a team colour.

The poet Ovid wrote how each charioteer, a slave, stood alone behind the starting gate, 'the horses panting impatiently against the bars of the gate'. The charioteer needed a great deal of skill to control his horses and to balance the small chariot while moving at high speed. There were often terrible crashes, especially at the turns: many charioteers were killed. However, a few successful racers became famous and earned enough money to buy their freedom.

The picture (left) is based on a mosaic (above left) and an ivory figure (above). A palm branch was given to the winning charioteer as a symbol of his victory.

A ROMAN MILECASTLE

By the 1st century AD, the Roman Empire had expanded and many new provinces had been conquered. This success came because the army was well organised, trained, equipped and disciplined. At the height of its power, the army had 29 legions, each of about 6,000 soldiers and craftsmen such as smiths and tent-makers. These were supported by units of foreign soldiers called auxiliaries.

The cavalry was a small but important part of the Roman army. Above and left are a bit (a mouth-piece for controlling a horse), a horseshoe, and a cavalryman's parade helmet.

Left is the tombstone of an auxiliary cavalryman from Thrace, Greece. It shows a cavalryman riding down a barbarian enemy.

Foot soldiers (right) were armed with a javelin (called a pilum) for throwing at the enemy. They then fought with a stabbing sword like the one on the left. Until the second century AD, soldiers were also issued with daggers (above, shown with its scabbard). Cavalry (above right) carried large spears and a longer sword.

Boots (above) were very important to a soldier. The boots had heavy hobnails to make the soles hard-wearing.

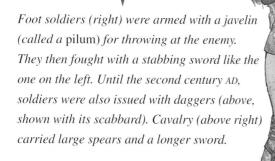

A soldier had to carry all his kit with him, including a palisade stake (which would be used to make a fence), a turf cutter, a trench digging tool, pick axe, bucket and mess (food) tin.

A soldier was responsible for his equipment. If something was lost or broken then the soldier had to pay to replace it.

The legionaries were citizens of Rome. They enlisted in the army for 25 years, after which they retired and received a pension or perhaps some land and a small villa. Some auxiliaries had been captured and forced to be in the army; others were volunteers. They looked forward to the day when they could leave the army, becoming a Roman citizen.

When they were away from their main bases, the legions built camps for the night. First they would dig a large ditch around the site, piling the earth to form a bank. Next the soldiers put up wooden stakes to make a protective fence, called a palisade, before pitching their tents for the night.

To mark the boundaries of the empire, the Romans built defensive walls, such as Hadrian's Wall in northern England. In the scene on the left we can see soldiers at a guard post on the wall. Mostly the soldiers did boring guard duties, such as watching traders cross the frontier. Occasionally there might be a raid across the border, perhaps to seize cattle. On the left we can see the milecastle under attack from Celtic warriors charging across the snow.

Along Hadrian's Wall in northern England there are the remains of several guard posts called milecastles (left). They were, as their name suggests, built one Roman mile (about 1,500 metres) apart.

Soldiers wore armour for protection. The armour was made of strips of metal. These strips or bands were either hinged or laced together with leather. This gave the soldiers good freedom of movement.

SIEGE!

ROMANIA AD 101

Every aspect of warfare was planned carefully by the army. In open battle, the Roman soldiers nearly always defeated their opponents. Armies of Celts, like the Germans and Dacians, fought as unruly mobs, yelling war cries as they charged the tight Roman formations. The Romans waited calmly before throwing their deadly javelins, then fought shoulder-to-shoulder, shield-to-shield, cutting down the enemy with their short stabbing swords.

Sometimes the Romans would have to lay siege to an enemy stronghold. The legionaries dug ditches and erected walls to keep the enemy contained, and to protect their own camps. Skilled craftsmen and ingenious engineers then built siege machines. There were battering rams for breaking down gates, and tall towers with a drawbridge on top so the soldiers could run on to the top of the walls. Catapults and ballistas threw stones or arrows with terrifying accuracy and deadly results.

The army looked after its wounded soldiers. Medical instruments included a surgical knife, a blunt probe, glass dropper, tweezers, hook, spatula, scalpel and forceps.

This gold medallion dating from AD 296 was found in France. It shows a galley ship and the freeing of London from rebels.

Trajan's column (above) was commissioned by the emperor Trajan to celebrate his defeat of the Dacians in what is now Romania. This scene shows legionaries building defences as they advance into Dacia.

Four-armed caltrops and iron spikes (below) were spread on the ground to stop cavalry attacks. They could inflict terrible injuries on horses. The metal spike was buried with only the barb sticking up.

These pieces from a ballista (left) were found in Romania. Many of Rome's enemies did not have weapons like the ballista and catapult shown in the scene.

Siege engines fired a variety of missiles, such as these catapult stones (below), rocks and large spears.

Each unit of the army had a standard (below right), which was taken out of the main camp only when the army marched into battle. The loss in battle of its eagle standard, called an aquila, *was a great humiliation for a Roman legion.*

The signal to attack, or retreat, would be given on war-horns like the one below.

Even though a siege could last for months, the Romans nearly always broke through. As the defences crumbled, the foot soldiers attacked. To protect themselves from volleys of stones, spears and arrows, most of the soldiers held their shields above their heads, overlapped to form a protective roof. The men at the sides held their shields to form walls. Advancing slowly, this 'tortoise' formation was hard to break up. The writer Sallust said of Marius, an army commander:

'He went outside the mantlets [protective shields], formed the tortoise-shield, and advanced to the wall.'

Once inside the defences, the Romans ruthlessly hunted down their foes.

GLOSSARY

**This list explains the meaning of some of the words
and terms used in the book.**

AN
AMPHORA

ATRIUM	The main reception area of a Roman home.
AMPHITHEATRE	A circular or oval building which was used for spectator sports such as animal and gladiator fights.
AMPHORA	A large two-handled pottery vessel used for storing goods.
ARCHAEOLOGIST	A person who finds and studies the remains of past cultures.
ARTEFACT	An object from the past that has been made by people.
AUXILIARIES	Soldiers of the Roman army who were not Roman citizens.
BALLISTA	A weapon similar to a crossbow, but much larger. It fired large stones or spears.
CAVALRY	Soldiers of the Roman army who fought on horseback. The cavalry were auxiliaries.
CELTS	The name given to native peoples of western and central Europe, including Britain and Gaul.
CHRISTIANITY	The belief in the life, death and teachings of Jesus Christ.
CITIZEN	A free person who had rights in their own city or region. At first, Roman citizens had to be born in Rome, but later other people in the empire could become Roman citizens.
DACIA	A country in the area that is now Romania. Dacia was conquered by the emperor Trajan in AD 101-106.
DENDRO-CHRONOLOGY	System of dating wood from the patterns of its annual growth rings. The system can date wood accurately to more than 7,000 years ago.
EMPEROR	Ruler of the Roman empire. The first emperor was Augustus, who reigned from 27 BC to AD 14.
FRESCO	A wall-painting that is painted directly onto plaster.
GLADIATORS	Slaves who were trained to fight in the amphitheatre. A gladiator who won many combats could earn his freedom.
GROMA	A surveying instrument used by the engineers of the army.
JAVELIN	A long, thin spear that was thrown at the enemy.
LEGION	A large unit of the Roman army, which contained approximately 5,000 soldiers plus craftsmen.
MILECASTLE	A small military stronghold, which usually protected a gateway through a defensive wall.
MOSAIC	A pattern or picture made out of tiny coloured pieces of stone or pottery called *tessarae*.
PATRICIANS	The Roman nobles, who were wealthy landowners. The ordinary free citizens were known as Plebeians.
POMPEII	An Italian town buried by ash from the volcano Vesuvius in AD 79.
PROVINCE	An area outside Italy that was ruled by the Romans.
RELIEF	A scene carved out of stone.

AUXILIARY
CAVALRY
PARADE
HELMET

A SLAVE
CHARIOTEER

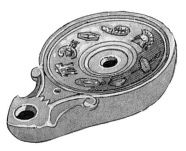

A Terracotta
LAMP

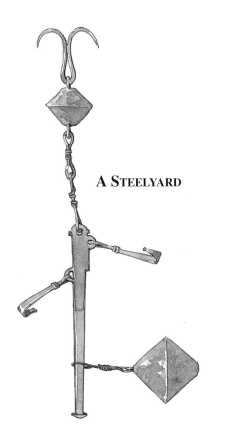

A Steelyard

Samian
Pottery

Samian	The common name for a form of red pottery made in Gaul.
Slaves	People who were owned by other people. Slaves had very few rights, but could be treated almost as part of the family: many educated Greek slaves were bought as tutors for Roman children, and some slaves eventually earned their freedom.
Steelyard	A device for weighing heavy objects.
Terracotta	Baked clay, used for making statuettes and pottery.
Tessarae	Small coloured stones used to make a mosaic.

KEY DATES

BC

753	The city of Rome is founded, according to legend. It is ruled by kings.
509	Rome becomes a Republic, ruled by people elected by Roman citizens.
340-280	Rome expands her lands in Italy, at the expense of the Etruscans, Samnites and the Celts of northern Italy.
264-146	Rome defeats the Carthaginians in three long wars, and sets up provinces in Spain, Greece, southern France and North Africa.
58-44	Julius Caesar conquers France (Gaul), then becomes ruler of Rome.
30	Egypt becomes the Roman province of Aegyptus.
27	The end of the Republic; Augustus becomes the first emperor.

AD

43-84	Conquest of Britain (Britannia).
70	Roman armies put down a revolt in Jerusalem in Judaea.
79	Mount Vesuvius erupts, burying the towns of Pompeii and Herculaneum in ash.
98-117	The reign of the emperor Trajan, who conquers Dacia. The empire is at its most powerful.
306-337	The reign of the emperor Constantine, who makes Constantinople the Christian capital and declares Christianity to be the official religion.
395	The empire is divided into two parts: the West, which is ruled from Rome, and the East, ruled from Constantinople.
406-476	The Western empire is overrun and collapses.
1453	The Eastern empire (Byzantium) collapses when Constantinople is captured by the Ottoman Turks.

QUOTATIONS

The quotations are taken from some of the many books, diaries and letters written by Romans. The lawyer and poet Juvenal (Decimus Junius Juvenalis) was very critical of the Roman upper classes. His *Satires*, written in the early second century AD, provide many realistic details of everyday life. Lucius Seneca was a philosopher and an adviser to the emperor Nero, who reigned from AD 54 to 68. Diodorus Siculus was a Greek historian who wrote a history of the world called the *Bibliotheca Historica*. The poet Ovid (Publius Ovidius Naso) trained as a lawyer but devoted his time to writing. The politician and historian Sallust (Gaius Sallustius Crispus) wrote about the general Marius, whom he had never met, many years after Marius' death. However, Sallust would have known about the 'tortoise' formation (page 29) because he had served in the army in Africa.

INDEX